Curt the Surfer

by Dan West
illustrated by Len Epstein

Practice Decodable 42

I0806508

McGraw Hill Education

Bothell, WA • Chicago, IL • Columbus, OH • New York, NY

MHEonline.com

Send all inquiries to:
McGraw-Hill Education
8787 Orion Place
Columbus, OH 43240

ISBN: 978-0-02-135442-9
MHID: 0-02-135442-1

Printed in China.

8 9 10 11 12 DSS 27 26 25 24 23

This is Curt.

Curt is at the hamburger stand.

Erma is with Curt. Erma can surf.
Erma tells Curt, "I am the best surfer."

"The surf is Curt's turf," blurts Curt.

Curt can surf.

Curt is a blur as he spins and turns.

Erma tells Curt, "The surf is Curt's turf."

"A hamburger is not Curt's turf!" adds Erma.